D0116604

Sexual Harassment

Sexual Harassment

A QUESTION OF POWER

JoAnn Bren Guernsey

LERNER PUBLICATIONS COMPANY
MINNEAPOLIS, MINNESOTA

Library of Congress Cataloging-in-Publication Data

Guernsey, JoAnn Bren.
    Sexual harassment / by JoAnn Bren Guernsey.
        p.   cm. — (Pro/Con)
    Includes bibliographical references and index.
    ISBN 0-8225-2608-5
    1. Sexual harassment of women—United States—Juvenile literature.
I. Title. II. Series
HQ1237.5.U6G84 1995
305.42—dc20   94-537
                                                                      CIP

Manufactured in the United States of America

1 2 3 4 5 6 I/S 00 99 98 97 96 95

Contents

A "NEW" SOCIAL ISSUE

1

K aty Lyle was a high school sophomore when a
friend told her about the graffiti he had seen
scrawled in the boys' bathroom. Along with other
sexually offensive messages, the graffiti said, "Katy Lyle is
a whore." Over the next year and a half, Katy and her parents notified school officials 16 times, but the graffiti was
not removed. In fact, it became more and more degrading. Katy was "scared to walk down the halls" because
male students frequently made humiliating comments
about her. Although she had been a straight-A student,
her grades fell and her social life declined.

Finally, Katy filed a complaint with her state's Department of Human Rights, claiming that her school district
had violated the law prohibiting sexual harassment,
broadly defined as unwanted sexual attention. By ignoring offensive and illegal behavior, Katy claimed, the school
had allowed a "hostile" environment to exist, which inter-
fered with her education.

The Department of Human Rights agreed with her. As
a result, the school district was ordered to post an official
sexual harassment policy, to remove graffiti every day,

Many women now enter the workforce—some in jobs traditionally held by men. In the U.S. Army, women can serve in most units, but not all.

and to award Katy $15,000 for "mental anguish." Experts believe this Duluth, Minnesota, school is the first in the United States to pay damages to a student. Katy is now 19 and in college, but she still has difficulty trusting people.[1]

History of the Conflict

Sexual harassment is nothing new; tension and discord between the sexes have probably always existed. As more and more women began to work outside the home, however, they took a closer look at some of the consequences of this tension—especially at the apparent inequality between men and women in the workplace. Women, for example, were barred from certain jobs. Also, they are often not paid as much as their male counterpart doing the same job. In 1964 the United States Congress passed the Civil Rights Act, which prohibits job discrimination because of a person's color, race, national origin, religion, or sex. Part of that law—Title VII—established a new federal agency, the EEOC (Equal Employment Opportunity Commission), to review various forms of job discrimination, including sex discrimination. But the issue of sexual harassment was not clearly identified until the mid-1970s, when the women's movement had become a strong force in the United States.

The modern movement for women's rights, which began in the early 1960s, sought social and political change and greater equality for women in the family, in the workplace, and in political life. In 1974 Carmita Wood became one of the movement's first heroines. Wood was a 44-year-old mother of four who had been working as an administrative assistant to a prominent scientist. She had also been fighting off his sexual advances for so long that she became physically ill and quit her job. She filed for and was promptly denied unemployment insurance. She also lost her case on appeal.[2]

By this time, however, activists in the women's movement had rallied around her. They found legal help for her and circulated questionnaires that revealed an astonishing number of women with similar experiences. Many women testified about their experiences at government hearings. The ultimate result was that the EEOC began to hear cases and decide in favor of a few women who sued harassing employers for sex discrimination.

Slowly, and with little publicity, case law—law established by a judge's decision after hearing a case—began to broaden the definition of behavior found to be in violation of Title VII. New cases extended the law beyond situations in which a boss required a woman to have sex with him (or her) in order to keep a job or get a promotion. The concept of a "hostile work environment" began to take shape. It covered harassment by coworkers, and also drew attention to many subtle forms of intimidating, demeaning behavior such as nude pinups on walls and dirty jokes.

In November 1980, the EEOC finally issued a set of federal guidelines. They stated clearly that sexual activity as a condition of employment or promotion was a violation of Title VII of the 1964 Civil Rights Act. Beyond that, they stated that an intimidating, hostile, or offensive work environment was also a violation. Verbal abuse alone was enough to create such an environment. The guidelines also encouraged companies to develop sexual harassment policies, inform all employees about them, and enforce them when violations occurred.[3]

The Hill-Thomas Controversy

The public paid little attention to sexual harassment, however, until October 1991. Sexual harassment then became an everyday expression and the topic of heated debate. People—males as well as females—got angry, and tension between the sexes grew during the televised battle between Anita Hill and Clarence Thomas.

President George Bush nominated Clarence Thomas to replace Thurgood Marshall on the United States Supreme Court, the highest court in the country. Since the position is a lifetime appointment, potential justices must undergo a Senate Judiciary Committee hearing to determine if they are qualified for the job.

Questions of character as well as judicial experience are important during these hearings. After all, the deci-

United States Supreme Court justice nominee Clarence Thomas
testified before the Senate Judiciary Committee during his confirmation hearing. He insisted he was not guilty of sexual harassment.

sions handed down by the Supreme Court are often of a
moral nature—determining right from wrong. Is legal
abortion, for instance, a constitutional right, or is it murder? Is the death penalty cruel and unusual punishment?
Such difficult decisions are supposed to be made with in-
tellectual attention directed strictly by the written law of
the land, but decisions are made by human beings.

Early in the Thomas confirmation proceedings, a law
professor named Anita Hill came forward to accuse
Thomas of sexually harassing her when she worked for
him (ironically, at the EEOC) 10 years earlier. She accused
him of making unwanted sexual advances and offensive
remarks regarding pornography he had supposedly seen.
She did not claim that her career had been threatened by
her resistance to his advances, but she had been certain,

at the time, that she would have risked her job by reporting him. Her accusations centered primarily around the hostile work environment she felt he had created.

The hearings were televised nationally, and millions of Americans sat transfixed in front of their TVs. Viewers witnessed hours of vivid testimony. They saw two dignified, articulate, black professionals being judged by a panel of 14 white male senators.

Did Thomas hound Hill for a date? Did he make remarks to her about the size of his penis and about his own sexual prowess? Did he describe pornographic films he'd seen showing women being raped and engaging in sex with animals? Was Hill hospitalized at one point because of the stress in her work environment?

Thomas adamantly denied every accusation, claiming he had never even asked Hill for a date. He expressed shock, surprise, sadness, and pain upon learning of the

Oklahoma law professor Anita Hill claimed that Clarence Thomas had sexually harassed her when he was her boss at the Equal Employment Opportunity Commission during the early 1980s.

charges against him, especially since he felt he had befriended Hill and helped advance her career. Convinced he was a victim of a racially motivated attack, he refused to "play to the worst stereotypes we have about black men in this country." He angrily denounced the hearings as "a high-tech lynching for uppity blacks" and said he would have preferred "an assassin's bullet to this kind of living hell."[4]

After days of emotion and drama, it came down to her word against his, and Thomas was the one who prevailed. He took his seat on the U.S. Supreme Court.

The story did not the end with the hearings, however. By coming forward as she did, putting herself under often humiliating public scrutiny, Anita Hill came to rep-

After days of emotional testimony in the Senate Judiciary Committee, the question of sexual harassment came down to the word of Clarence Thomas against the word of Anita Hill. Thomas, standing at the far left, was confirmed.

resent thousands of women, previously silent, who had endured similar (and worse) episodes of sexual harassment. The hearings ended, but so did the silence. Widespread publicity revealed harassment to be an apparently common form of sex discrimination.

The Aftermath

Professor Hill's accusations of Clarence Thomas had a dramatic effect on sexual harassment charges filed with the federal EEOC. The number of charges jumped from 6,892 in 1991 to almost 13,000 in 1993.[5] These numbers are still small, however, considering studies reporting that as many as 45 percent of the nation's 58 million employed women experience sexual harassment at work sometime during their careers.[6] Fear of losing their jobs discourages most women from fighting back. In addition, it is likely that potential complainants were more discouraged than encouraged by the results of the Thomas hearings. The Senate did confirm Thomas to the Supreme Court, after all. And public opinion was split—many Americans believed Thomas, not Hill, and expressed outrage at the humiliation he underwent during the proceedings.

One result of the Hill-Thomas controversy was in the political arena. Although not running for any office, Anita Hill became a powerful force in the politics of 1992, an election year. Many people (women *and* men) sharply criticized the way the Senate Judiciary Committee treated her during the hearings. A few even compared her to Rosa Parks, whose refusal to sit in the back of the bus sparked the civil rights movement.

The events of October 1991 seemed to have provoked increased interest and participation in politics among women, many of whom vowed to support whatever candidates (usually Democrats) they perceived as more sympathetic to so-called women's issues, or even to support female candidates solely because of their gender. Many women declared that it was time to stop minimizing the importance of sexual harassment.

Carol Mosely Braun was among the women candidates who entered politics because of the way Anita Hill was treated during the hearings. Braun won the Illinois Senate race and became the first black woman elected to the U.S. Senate. Lynn Yeakel entered the Senate race in Pennsylvania to replace Senator Arlen Specter, one of the most aggressively anti-Hill members of the Judiciary panel. Yeakel narrowly lost the election, but voters nationwide cheered her campaign's messages.[7]

Organizations that raise money for women candidates reported a surge in contributions during early 1992. Some women's leaders claimed that because of the reaction of the committee and the public to Hill's charge of sexual harassment, the issue went well beyond whether Thomas was fit to serve on the Supreme Court. Most women could not quite shake off the image of a female being judged by a group of male lawmakers who could not seem to understand anything about what she'd experienced. A slogan emerged that seemed, for many women, to sum up men's attitudes: "They just don't get it."

An Overreaction?

In the months following the Thomas hearings, however, many people wondered if the American public was overreacting to the issue. They expressed concern about doing irreparable harm to male/female relationships, about

The line between flirtation and harassment is sometimes unclear. Often, much depends on the situation and the people involved.

undermining trust between the sexes, which could make it difficult for women and men to work together. Many people wonder what it will take to avoid any risk of illegal behavior in the workplace. Will men and women be required to relate to one another like machines?

Not all people are offended by the game-playing that can occur between the sexes, including that common expression of male-female attraction known as flirtation. If a misunderstanding occurs, it can usually be cleared up easily when the offender is told, firmly and clearly, to stop. But sexual harassment goes beyond flirtation and cannot always be avoided or easily handled. Abuses of power occur frequently, and the results can be devastating.

Sexual harassment is not easy to define. Sometimes the boundaries between acceptable and unacceptable behavior seem to vary with the circumstances and the individuals involved. If an employer sexually assaults an employee, or makes it clear that the person's job depends on sexual favors, his or her behavior is blatantly offensive and illegal. But other situations are not so clear.

One video used in sexual harassment seminars shows the following scene:

Woman (at a photocopying machine): "Sorry, I'll be out of your way in a second."

Man (leaning on counter): "Take your time. I'm enjoying the view."

What do *you* think about this exchange? Obviously, the man's tone, facial expression, and body language have to be considered, but is it possible that the woman might be only mildly annoyed by his remark? Is it even possible she might be flattered? Would there be any problem at all if it had been a woman making this remark to a man instead?

Certainly a range of behavior exists, all the way from the innocent gesture or remark to the brutal assault. But many feminists put the entire range of behavior in the context of male power. According to Boston University psychology professor Frances Grossman:

> From the guys who wink on the street to the biology professor who tells a sexist joke in class, to the guy who says, 'Hey, baby, let's go out,' to the guy who rapes—all are of a piece in their role of disempowering women. Men say these are not related behaviors. Flirting and jokes are fine, and rape is bad, they say. But increasingly, sociologists say they all send the same disempowering message to women.[8]

This kind of viewpoint outrages many men—and women as well. Does judging all men, essentially, as "pigs" provide any constructive basis for change and for getting along together? And what about those cases when men are the victims of sexual harassment? Is such "disempowerment" justified in those cases?

Losing Ground

The current sexual harassment laws also have some unintended effects. Some employers are afraid to hire women for fear of facing an expensive lawsuit, or maybe even being forced out of business. After so many years of fighting for equal opportunities, women hardly need yet another reason to be overlooked for jobs. And how likely are men who do employ women to give them any special attention if they fear being accused of sexual harassment?

Some people accuse civil rights laws of coddling women and putting them back "on the pedestal." And, as business owner and feminist activist Sarah McCarthy points out in an opinion piece for *Forbes* magazine, a pedestal is "as confining as any other small place." McCarthy goes on to urge feminist leaders not to "trivialize the women's movement" by flooding the courts with questionable claims of sexual harassment. "We women," she says, "are not as delicate and powerless as you think. We do not want victim status in the workplace. Don't try to foist it on us."[9]

Nobody wants to go back to the way it used to be for women. Sex discrimination and harassment in everyday life are clearly problems that need continuing attention and new solutions. But this book represents an effort shared by many of both sexes to go beyond the "us-against-them" mentality and examine the issue of sexual harassment in all its complexity.

2
MALE/FEMALE ROLES

G ender gap. Battle of the sexes. Domestic violence. Describing male/female relationships seems to require an increasingly combative vocabulary. Such phrases as *male oppression* and *feminist male bashing* are becoming almost as commonplace as terms like *friendship, romance,* and *love.* The phrase *women's liberation* has been tossed around for the last two decades. Liberation from what? From whom? The words imply an enslavement. Men are beginning to see this as an accusation and to say, "Hey, wait a minute . . . ."

In a 1990 poll conducted by the Roper Organization, 70 to 80 percent of men polled expressed contentment with their lives and with the way they and their wives shared family and household responsibilities. Most men also said they believed that the women's movement has improved life for women. However, at least half of the women questioned in the same poll expressed resentment—even rage—about the same family and work issues. The female respondents tended to depict men as selfish, self-centered, and not interested in home life. The Roper poll's conclusion was that women are "even angrier with men than they were 20 years ago."[1]

On June 18, 1983, Sally Ride was America's first woman astronaut to go into outer space—one of many firsts for women during the 70s and 80s.

Why are women so angry? Are they really worse off than they were in the 1960s and 1970s, when the women's movement emerged? In most ways, no. What has changed, many experts agree, is that women have come to *expect* more from their relationships with men as well as in their own lives. They are far less likely to tolerate

Geraldine Ferraro became the first woman representing a major political party to run for vice president of the United States in 1984. Walter Mondale ran for president.

sexism quietly. Added to this impatience is the growing alarm about rape, wife-battering, and other forms of violence against women.

As *Newsweek* writer Laura Shapiro pointed out after the Clarence Thomas hearings, "The anger ignited by Anita Hill's charges had been smoldering for years, fed not only by the common experience of sexual harassment but all the outrages large and small that make this country a radically different place for women than it is for men."[2] And the outrage remains, for most women, unfocused, with no specific culprit, which adds to their sense of helplessness. Apparently, this sense of powerlessness, mixed with fear, is profoundly disturbing to women.

Activism has clearly made a difference to women. For example, more than a third of this century's women's

rights legislation passed during the 1970s, when lobby-
ing groups such as the National Organization for Women
(NOW) became active. Nearly every field could boast its
"first woman" this or that—from U.S. astronaut Sally Ride
to Supreme Court Justice Sandra Day O'Connor to vice
presidential candidate Geraldine Ferraro. In other fields
such as medicine and the law, the percentages of female
graduates and practitioners climbed dramatically. The
number of women doctors, for instance, more than dou-
bled between 1975 and 1985.[3] But has it been enough?

As recently as 1974, Kathryn Kirschbaum, the mayor
of Davenport, Iowa, had to get her husband's signature
on a credit card application. And in 1984, Clarence Pen-
dleton, of the U.S. Civil Rights Commission, called equal
pay for equal work "the looniest idea since Looney Tunes
came on the screen."[4]

What happened during the 1980s? Many involved in
the women's movement claim that much of the economic and legal progress women made during the 1970s
got stalled dramatically during the Reagan/Bush years of
the 1980s. They point out that agencies such as the
EEOC were understaffed and underfunded. Furthermore,
the conservative appointments to the U.S. Supreme
Court by presidents Ronald Reagan and George Bush
brought about a reversal of many judicial decisions on
women's issues. In June 1989, for example, the Court
made civil rights rulings that established new legal barri-
ers that made it far more difficult to demonstrate sex discrimination in court.[5]

During the 1980s, even the word *feminism* suddenly
seemed suspect. "Women's libbers" were ridiculed as bra
burners with hairy legs—an image referring to widely

publicized, symbolic actions taken by some protesters during the 1960s. Many people began to say that the women's movement was dead. A happy "postfeminist" American woman was supposed to have emerged. This image began to take hold in the media even though many people complained that she looked just like her prefeminist sisters, "give or take a briefcase."[6]

Even if conditions are better for women now, actual equality is more an illusion than a fact. On average, women earn about 60 cents for every dollar earned by men—same jobs, different earning power. The disparity is even higher between college-educated men and women. Furthermore, women tend to be laid off or fired in greater numbers than men. Isn't this against the law? Yes, and women can sue. But at the same time that sex-discrimination complaints were pouring into the EEOC, President Reagan cut the agency's budget in half.[7] Barbara Otto, a spokeswoman for 9to5, a nationwide advocacy group for working women, says, "You can be fired because you have a sick child, you can be fired because you're pregnant."[8] And poverty is increasingly becoming a female phenomenon. More than one in three families headed by single mothers rank in the bottom fifth of this nation's income distribution.[9]

Education researchers say the problem of disparity begins long before women enter the workforce; it appears to begin in school. A report issued in 1992 by the American Association of University Women says that "girls get less attention in school, face biased tests and textbooks, and are steered away from math and science courses that would make them more competitive in today's high-tech world."[10] This bias occurs even though

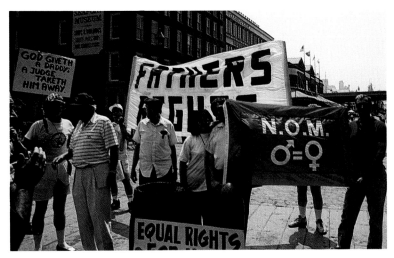

A growing men's movement has sprouted in response to the women's movement. Child custody in divorce proceedings is one of its goals.

most teachers are women. Boys appear to come into school demanding more attention, and they generally get it. The result is that many girls leave school with lower self-esteem and less confidence than boys.

The panic about women's rights is not, however, universal. Many women are offended by all the "whining and moaning" about feminism being dead. For many, the original message of the women's movement was, essentially, for women to get tougher and stop being "doormats." And some experts say women often become victims by acting like victims.

And what about the male point of view? Many men point out that they would be delighted to give up some of their "advantages." The role of primary breadwinner is a burden to many men, as are the expectations that men should risk death on battlefields and that they should keep their emotions hidden. A burgeoning men's movement fights for—among other rights—equal consideration regarding child custody in divorce proceedings.

One of the biggest controversies in this issue of male/female equality revolves around the question of why and how much the sexes differ from each other. The women's movement tended, in the past, to claim that males and females are the same except in the ability to bear children. In this view, inequality is produced by cultural brainwashing. Many experts cite evidence that the biological differences between men and women are too powerful to be overlooked or overcome. Culture plays a part in how we look at ourselves and each other, but many gender differences seem to be rooted in the human brain.

Undeniably, males and females differ dramatically in terms of hormones. Women menstruate and can have children. Men produce the sperm that can unite with a woman's egg. The hormones associated with the reproductive function—testosterone in men and estrogen in women—affect our behavior. Testosterone, for example, has been blamed (or applauded) for making men more aggressive.

Women, on the other hand, may experience physical and emotional changes related to their menstrual cycles. Premenstrual syndrome (PMS) is a fairly common phenomenon. Although PMS is rarely a major problem, some statistics show an apparent relationship between PMS and suicides and homicides committed by women.[11] Some people justify choosing a man over a woman for a position of power because they believe her judgment or performance could be affected by her cycles.

Gender roles, as related to work, are as ancient as human life itself. In the past, when survival needs, such as food and shelter, required maximum physical strength and aggression, the division of labor was naturally drawn between those who could bear children and those who could best provide food and shelter for them. In the not-too-distant past, when men were the providers and women were primarily childbearers and homemakers, women came to be viewed as dependents, even as possessions. Many women (especially the very wealthy) were protected, sheltered, and offered a life of luxury and leisure. But the price was high; women tended not to achieve any significant degree of independence or status apart from their family.

Now, of course, women share in work responsibilities, and they are less likely to be defined solely as wives and mothers. Women are not as isolated from public life and lead far more independent lives. But in many families, women still carry a heavier burden of household chores no matter what else they do. Furthermore, traditional gender roles do not disappear instantly just because their economic roots have disappeared. In other words, old habits die hard.[12]

Sex discrimination is a continuing problem that, despite progress, is anything but solved. But it is important to distinguish between sex discrmination and sexual harassment. Sex discrimination is a much broader term that covers all forms of gender-based inequality such as differences in pay and benefits. Charges of sexual harassment, however, should be limited to those cases in which a woman (or man) feels intimidated or threatened by unwanted sexual attention.

The role of women has changed dramatically over the past few decades. Women have become less isolated and more independent. We see more working mothers since few women can afford to stay home to be full-time homemakers.

The remainder of this book will deal with sexual harassment in many different forms and under differing circumstances. In terms of male/female relationships, however, the explosion of interest in sexual harassment has had widespread repercussions. Fewer cases of blatant sexual harassment will be allowed to slide by, but it is also possible that too many false or at least weak accusations will result in trivializing more serious victimization.

But perhaps the biggest question in this controversy is, who decides what constitutes sexual harassment? According to some women's rights activists, the answer is simple: Women get to define what is and is not offensive, and the law should comply. If a woman says an incident happened, it happened. After all, who else is in a better position to define sexual harassment than the victim? According to sociologist Susan Marshall, men "don't understand that caged feeling . . . but women know what sexual harassment is. It's when your neck hairs stand up, when you feel like you're being stalked."[13]

Others disagree. Current definitions of sexual harassment are vague, some say even useless. What *is* a hostile work environment anyway? Is it sexual harassment when a man displays a photo of a nude model in his private work space? Is it sexual harassment to tell a dirty joke within earshot of a female? In a few recent cases, the answer from the courts was *yes*. What about the constitutional right of these men to freedom of expression?

Equally troubling, what if women are telling off-color jokes, discussing menstruation, or in other ways making their male coworkers uncomfortable? Is the work environment, in that case, somehow less hostile just because it is created by women?

3

SEXUAL HARASSMENT IN THE WORKPLACE

Jane is 16 years old and always broke. In spite of her C average at school, she talks her parents into letting her take a part-time job at a nearby fast-food restaurant. Her parents don't like the idea and warn her that she must prove herself able to handle all the pressures of school *and* job, or they'll make her quit the job.

Within the first few days at her job, Jane becomes uneasy about her manager, Bob. He keeps staring at her, commenting on her legs and breasts. Soon he starts touching her and pressuring her for a date. Clearly, for Bob, a date does not mean going to a concert or out to dinner. Jane comes home from work every day feeling dirty—defiled.

If she just quietly quits this job and tries to get another, her parents will want to know why she would quit after only a few days. She doesn't dare tell her parents about the situation. They didn't trust her to handle things before she took the job. What will they think of her now? They'll probably think she flirted with Bob and brought the problem on herself. Or maybe they won't believe her. They might think that she's just imagining things, that she's too young and immature to handle life in the workforce. After all, Bob is well respected in the community. He even received an award recently for being an excellent role model for young people who want to be successful in business.

Threatened with being fired and given a terrible recommendation, Jane finally gives in to Bob, and they start dating. He tells her that he knows she wants it. He can tell by the way she dresses, the way she walks. Jane keeps quiet about what's happening to her, and her life begins to disintegrate. This behavior pattern goes on for several months until Jane finally quits in desperation, too ashamed to tell anyone what's happened. Bob hires her replacement, another young woman eager for money and independence.

This fictitious story is based on those of many teenagers who have had terrible first job experiences. How do you suppose this kind of experience affects the future of girls like Jane?

Struggling with Definitions

Debates about what is or is not sexual harassment get most heated when discussing the concept of a "hostile working environment." This phrase is meant to cover any sexual behavior that is unwelcome and makes it hard for a worker to do her or his job. The courts look more at the victim's reaction than the harasser's intent. In other words, even if a person is creating a hostile environment without knowing it, he or she is still guilty of sexual harassment and may face legal consequences.[1]

In the courts, the definition of sexual harassment seems simpler than what many people experience in real life. Sexual harassment is not about the specific action of asking for a date, complimenting someone's appearance, or even telling an off-color joke. Rather, it is an abuse of *power.* When a person is made to feel vulnerable—personally and professionally—by a superior's sexual attention, she or he may be experiencing harassment. "This is not automatically a male-female issue," says Wendy Redi Crisp, director of the National Association of Female Executives, the largest women's professional association in the country. "We define this issue as economic intimidation."[2] In other words, she's saying, harassment threatens a person's sense of financial well-being.

Sexual harassment—unwanted sexual attention—is an abuse of power.

But such intimidation does not always come from the boss; the concept of a hostile work environment covers behavior by coworkers as well. And customers or clients can also try to intimidate someone into sexual favors, sending the message that their offensive behavior must be tolerated or they will take their business elsewhere.

Men as well as women are victims of sexual harassment, targeted both by male and female employers, coworkers, and clients. According to some estimates, the number of victimized men is about one-third that of women, but sexual harassment consultants say that less than five percent of the victims are men.[3] The exact number is impossible to determine because men are far less likely than women to report harassment. As difficult as it is for a woman to talk about harassment, it's usually even more difficult for a man. "He tends to get laughed out of the room," says Susan L. Webb, a Seattle management consultant who specializes in sexual harassment. "We have this underlying belief that men should be sexually available at all times—and like it."[4]

Invading the "Locker Room"

The risk for women is highest when they break into fields once dominated by men. Male coworkers often try to make the women uncomfortable by turning the workplace into a locker room. Essentially they're saying, "You wanted equality—I'm going to give it to you with a vengeance."

Police officers Lindsey Browne-Allison and Melissa Clerkin presented evidence to a jury in 1991 that their male-dominated police department regularly ridiculed women through obscene language and behavior. Clerkin says she was called a lesbian and once found a penis-shaped vibrator in her patrol car. Browne-Allison says male officers talked explictly about sex acts and urinated outdoors in her presence.[5]

The jury awarded these two women $3.1 million dollars, but the male officers involved never received any kind of discipline. They view the case as a big joke. The women, on the other hand, lost their careers as police officers, and one of them lost her marriage as well while fighting the case. They both have been left with emotional scars.

When construction worker Diane Joyce received her training to drive bobtail trucks, the men she worked with kept changing their instructions, and one gave her driving "tips" that nearly blew up the engine. In the yard the men kept the ladies' room locked, and on the road they wouldn't stop to let her use a bathroom. She recalls one superior telling her, "You wanted a man's job; you learn to pee like a man."[6]

In May 1991, Dr. Frances Conley, a leading neurosurgeon, quit her 25-year teaching position at Stanford University because of harassment from fellow physicians. She claims to have put up with male surgeons caressing her legs under the operating table, being called "honey," and being accused of having premenstrual syndrome when she engaged in arguments with men. When she found out that female medical students were having the same problems, Dr. Conley resigned in protest. She eventually returned to her teaching post, but only after bringing the issue of sexual harassment into the open at Stanford and seeing to it that officials were addressing the problem.[7]

As women move into jobs traditionally held by men, such as construction and law enforcement, they often encounter sexual harassment.

Lisa Olson, a sports reporter for the *Boston Herald,* was sexually harassed in the locker room of the New England Patriots. The National Football League fined the team a total of $72,500 for the incident, but that did not solve Olson's harassment problems.

For months, Boston sportswriter Lisa Olson received hate mail—even death threats—for having complained about her treatment when conducting an interview in a locker room. Three members of the New England Patriots football team had allegedly gathered around her, making obscene remarks. The players were naked. She had reported the incident to her editor at the *Boston Herald,* but she did not file a sexual harassment lawsuit until much later, after television and other newspapers got wind of the situation and her misery escalated. Still trying to cover various sporting events, she was harassed and threatened by fans who chanted her name and jostled and touched her. The owner of the Patriots team made jokes about her, then apologized, then joked again.

Meanwhile, the team management had done nothing about the incident in the locker room, so Lisa filed a lawsuit. When the players involved and the management were fined, her on-the-job problems got even worse. Patriot fans poured beer on her, spit on her head, spray-painted "Bitch" on her house, slashed her tires, and sent more obscene, threatening letters. She finally decided not only to leave Boston, but to leave the country and write for another newspaper in a foreign country. She will probably not do sportswriting again.[8]

A solution for some women in male-dominated jobs is to shed as much of their femininity as possible in order to fit in. A female stand-up comic who works in comedy clubs says, "The minute I get in, I become one of the guys. I've got to take my breasts off and talk from the head up and slap everybody around. I become this de-sexualized creature so that we can all work together."[9]

New arrivals from the United States Army's 24th Infantry listen for their orders after arriving at a port during the Gulf War.

Tailhook

Women in the military are at particular risk of sexual harassment, and apparently of having their complaints ignored or turned against them. Women make up less than 11 percent of the nation's 1.6 million military personnel—a distinct minority. Furthermore, if military women are harassed, assaulted, or even raped, they do not have the same options available to them as civilians. Their superior officers—usually male and often part of the problem—have complete authority. A woman in the military who fights off sexual attention from a male counterpart also runs the risk of being accused of homosexuality, an accusation that could end her career.

This tolerance of harassment in the military was dramatically altered, however, by shocking revelations early in 1992. Complaints flooded the Senate Armed Services Committee from dozens of military women who had been harassed, raped, or sexually assaulted while on duty, including those who had served in the Persian Gulf War. Fear of retaliation had kept women silent for years, but suddenly the situation changed.

On September 7, 1991, navy and marine aviators gathered in a Las Vegas hotel for the annual convention of the Tailhook Association, an independent group of active and retired aviators. What began as a party, however, turned into one of the worst scandals in naval history. At least 50 women (many of them navy officers) were forced to "run a gauntlet" (run between a double file of men) along a hotel corridor. The women were manhandled, bitten, and humiliated by drunken pilots. When the women first reported the incident, the navy chose to ignore the charges.

Why? As explained by Charles Moskos, a military sociologist at Northwestern University, "Subjecting these guys to classes in sexual harassment is like telling them not to smoke or drink. You can't oversocialize them because that might even drive out the best pilots."[10] Also, the tone at Tailhook was set at a workshop earlier in the evening when 2,000 male aviators jeered women officers who asked about their futures in naval aviation. Nobody representing the top naval brass tried to bring order to the workshop or side with the women.[11]

The Tailhook scandal eventually cost Secretary of the Navy H. Lawrence Garrett III his job, and other allegations of sexual harassment began to receive attention. But after months of investigation and hearings, not a single accused man had been disciplined. Lieutenant Paula Coughlin, one of the young women who had been mauled in the hotel, and the first to come forward with an official complaint, ended up resigning from the navy. She said that Tailhook "and the covert attacks on me that followed have stripped me of my ability to serve."[12]

A few other women, however, have found that the Tailhook scandal and its aftermath have helped expose sex-biased policies. The effort to correct sexually discriminating policies has, in some cases, opened up opportunities to women that had been previously denied, especially the chance to become combat pilots. According to former navy officials, Tailhook exposed biases and shook up resistance to change of all kinds. Educational programs, for instance, have been developed and are now required for all recruits. This crucial new part of training is aimed at making the mixed-gender assignments in the military safer and more comfortable for everyone.[13]

Admiral Frank Kelso announces his early resignation as Chief of Naval Operations as a result of Tailhook. He said, "I have become the lightning rod for Tailhook . . . and the lightning keeps striking."

The "Reasonable Woman" Judgment

The sexual harassment controversy has focused almost exclusively on criticizing men for behavior that some women say is not only ugly but extremely common. The sexual harassment laws have changed in response to feminist demands to broaden the definition of harassment. Yet most women remain unaware of their rights or are afraid to exercise them. "Women are subjected to a barrage of sexual innuendo, pictures, and verbal abuse, and most don't have the vaguest idea that they don't have to put up with it," says Sheila Kuel of the California Women's Law Center.[14]

But is sexual harassment anything an accuser says it is? Isn't it true that some people are more sensitive than others? If so, does the definition of sexual harassment

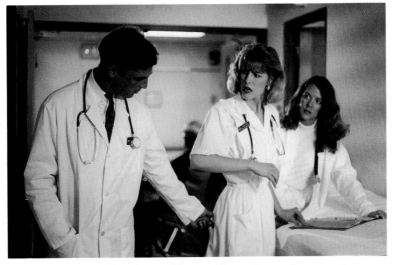

Men and women often have different ideas about what constitutes sexual abuse.

have to cover everything even potentially offensive to the most sensitive among us?

In a landmark 1991 ruling, the Ninth U.S. Distict Court in California ruled that the law covers any remark or behavior that a "reasonable woman" would find to be a problem. It also acknowledged that a woman's perception might be very different from a man's. Judge Robert Beezer wrote that "conduct that many men consider unobjectionable may offend many women." He noted that because women are much more likely to be victims of rape and sexual assault, they have a "stronger incentive to be concerned with sexual behavior." Furthermore, men are more likely to view sexual conduct as harmless.[15]

Studies lend support to this finding. One study has found that most men would be flattered if a woman propositioned them at work, while a majority of women said they would be offended by such behavior from men. Another survey by *Redbook* magazine and the *Harvard Business Review* indicated that 24 percent of the women and only 8 percent of the men believed that a man looking intently at a female worker was harassment.[16]

How, then, can people decide on what constitutes appropriate behavior? One sexual harassment sensitivity training program recommends that men ask themselves, "Would I want my mother, sister, or daughter exposed to this?"[17]

But how realistic is it to try to stop all rude and annoying behavior by making it illegal? And should corporations be forced to live under the tyranny of a few hypersensitive employees? Obviously, nobody should have to face a day at work feeling like they have to run a sexual gauntlet, but is it reasonable for women—or men—to expect a perfect work environment, free of all forms of offensive behavior?

A Perfect World?

Feminism is often blamed for creating unrealistic expectations in women who have taken jobs outside the home for the first time. Those Americans—women as well as men—who have been in the workplace the longest may have a slightly different understanding of life's realities. Those who have had no choice but to work in order to support a family know that, while work has its rewards, it also can create an atmosphere that is anything but pleasant. The unpleasantness is more likely to have sexual undercurrents for women, but many people question why this should be considered any worse than the uncertainties, frustrations, and humiliations that men encounter. The harsh reality is that talent is not always appreciated. Loyalty and hard work are not always rewarded.

White males who are often accused of being hostile to women's rights are defending themselves in the name of fairness. "If I were a woman or a minority," one might say, "I would have legal recourse when my boss treats me badly. I can match any sexually harassed woman's horror story with several of my own. But there's nothing I can do because I'm white and male. Why is harassment considered worse when it's based on gender or race? Why should women demand special treatment? Is this the meaning of equality?"

Furthermore, annoyances from the world outside the workplace are likely to seep inside as well. Sexual innuendo and tasteless jokes are common in the media—television, movies, radio, music, etc. Should an employer, then, be held liable because the same things bother someone in his or her office?[18]

In school and at work, people still have to fight against double standards—rules and expectations that work one way for men and another way for women. A woman is still more likely than a man, for example, to miss work because of a sick child at home. Consequently, the fact that she is a mother can have an impact (though unstated and subtle) on whether she is considered for promotion.

But it is not just women who complain of double standards. Men have come to feel they have to be careful about what they ask women to do. Such domestic tasks as making coffee used to be routinely taken care of by female workers. Now, of course, if a man assumes that a female secretary or female executive will make and serve coffee, he can be accused of sexual discrimination. But in many workplaces, especially where men are in the minority, it is not uncommon for traditionally male chores such as heavy lifting to fall to the men. Isn't this the equivalent of asking a woman to make coffee?

Fighting Back

Some experts say that male-female tensions will ease only if women who believe they are being harassed confront the problem directly. As Camille Paglia, author and critic of modern feminism, says, "Women allow themselves to become victims when they don't take responsibility. If getting the guy to stop means putting a heel in his crotch, then just do it. Don't complain about it 10 years later."[19] But fighting back is rarely as simple as telling the harasser to stop, and taking direct action can be complicated by the victim's own feelings.

Victims have to decide, then, not only if they're being harassed, but also if they should do something about it—and, if so, what they should do. For many women the decision about whether to take official action is an economic one. Getting fired may seem like too high a price for dignity or peace of mind.

Furthermore, it may be financially impossible to pursue a case. The EEOC does provide free legal help, but only for the few cases it chooses to take to court. Usually women have to hire attorneys themselves. Fees are often very high because the cases are so difficult to win and the settlements are relatively low.[20] The few harassment victims who do file complaints often find they have to quit their jobs anyway, because the conflict can make the work environment unbearable.

Is expecting a man in the workplace to lift heavy packages any different than assuming a woman will make the coffee?

Most women end up suffering in silence, because it's easier than fighting sexual harassment. "Many strong, successful professional women have made conscious decisions to ignore the sexual harassment in their offices because they know that as soon as they complained, there would be 50 others waiting to take their jobs," says author Naomi Wolf. She adds that it was easier for feminist pioneers to fight back against abuse because they had everything to gain and nothing to lose.[21]

Many women depend on male mentors—powerful men who have taken them "under their wing" to teach them and help them advance in their careers. If the mentorship system is at risk because of increased suspicion between the sexes, will fewer women attain their goals?

Professional relationships can be very complex, especially for ambitious women, and this fact may help answer a question often raised during the Thomas-Hill hearings: Why did Anita Hill wait 10 years to make her complaints? Many women say that such delay is not only believable but typical. As stated by one woman who was harassed while in her 20s: "I was a kid. I was trying hard to succeed. I told myself that this is the time to work hard, to jump through hoops, not the time to be spitting in people's faces and saying, 'I won't put up with this.'"[22]

Women are pressing for more legal benefits and they are, in fact, winning more monetary compensation in sexual discrimination and harassment cases. Just a week after Clarence Thomas was confirmed to the Supreme Court, President Bush signed the Civil Rights Act of 1991—legislation he had vetoed a year earlier. This act permitted, for the first time, monetary damages for victims of job discrimination.

Putting Sexual Harassment Policies into Place

How is the average employer affected by this controversy? An employer's concern about the problem is one
of self-interest. Significant amounts of money are at stake.
Recent court rulings have held companies liable for their
employees' sexist behavior—even if management was
unaware of it and had all the appropriate anti-harassment
policies in place. Therefore, more and more companies
offer videos and seminars on sexual harassment and issue detailed guidelines for appropriate on-the-job interaction between men and women.

According to a recent survey by *Working Women* magazine, ignoring the issue costs a typical large company as
much as $6.7 million a year in absenteeism, turnover, and
lost productivity. Three-quarters of the firms surveyed
had established anti-harassment policies, 90 percent have
received complaints, and 64 percent admitted that most
of the complaints they heard were valid. In roughly 80
percent of the cases, the harasser was reprimanded and
one in five was fired.[23]

But the nature of these employer responsibilities brings
up another potential problem in this issue: Sexual harassment has become big business for consulting firms that
sell advice to worried companies in the form of seminars, videos, and encounter groups. In one year, Dupont
spent $450,000 on sexual harassment training programs
and materials.[24] Is it possible that sexual harassment consultants exaggerate the problem so they can continue to
profit from the controversy? How do they gather and use
"facts" about the problem?

The above statistics about the millions of dollars being
lost in productivity and low employee morale provide an

Many companies offer workshops and seminars to establish behavioral guidelines in an effort to avoid the problems associated with sexual harassment.

example of facts derived from sexual harassment consultants. Does this mean such information can be ignored? Is the whole sexual harassment problem a result of hype and hysteria? No. But many experts urge caution in evaluating the problem. It is just as easy to find statistics that show a decrease in sexual harassment in the last few years. For example, harassment cases brought before the EEOC dropped from 6,342 in 1984 to 5,694 in 1990; this occurred even though 17 percent more women held jobs in 1990.[25]

The "Bad Guy" Image

Men pay a high price for living in a society where there is so much sexual exploitation and where sexual matters are often not dealt with in a healthy, straightforward way. Many men have had the unsettling experience of walking behind a woman at night, and then—when she speeds up or crosses the street—realizing she is afraid of him.

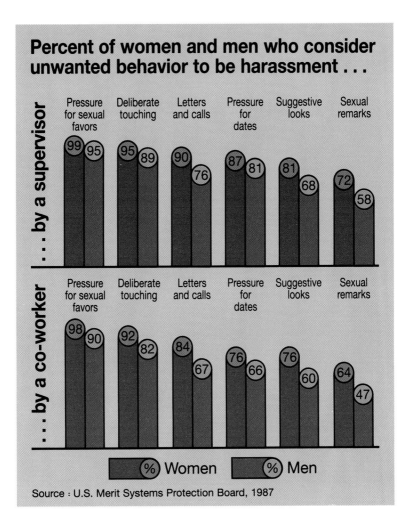

Percent of women and men who consider unwanted behavior to be harassment . . .

... by a supervisor

	Pressure for sexual favors	Deliberate touching	Letters and calls	Pressure for dates	Suggestive looks	Sexual remarks
Women	99	95	90	87	81	72
Men	95	89	76	81	68	58

... by a co-worker

	Pressure for sexual favors	Deliberate touching	Letters and calls	Pressure for dates	Suggestive looks	Sexual remarks
Women	98	92	84	76	76	64
Men	90	82	67	66	60	47

(%) Women   (%) Men

Source : U.S. Merit Systems Protection Board, 1987

The high rate of sexual crimes against women makes even innocent men sometimes seem like the "bad guys." It also makes them vulnerable to false accusations. The possibility that a gesture might be misunderstood or exaggerated is a serious concern. Are men being judged unfairly? Does the increase in the number of successful sexual harassment cases mean that more men—innocent as well as guilty—will be prosecuted?

In addition, men do not live in a vacuum. When someone they love—a girlfriend, wife, daughter, mother, friend—is the victim of a violent crime, the trauma extends to men as well. And it is much the same when women are mistreated at work.

Most men seem genuinely moved by the complaints of women, or at least consider themselves recent converts about the issue. Typical is William Schneider, a political analyst at the American Enterprise Institute, who said he had always known that sexual harassment existed, because he participated in it himself. But he did not know that women minded. "We thought if they weren't complaining, they must be happy."[26]

Other men, however, try to turn the issue of sexual harassment around. Fredric Hayward, the executive director of Men's Rights Inc. in Sacramento, California, looks at the same examples of sexual harassment in the workplace and finds a different victim. He admits that men may have more professional power, but he adds that women have sexual power and are just as likely to abuse this power as men are to abuse theirs. He says:

If I or a woman does not get a job because a female competitor displays more enticing cleavage, then what are we victims of? If I or a woman does not get a promotion because a female competitor has an affair with our boss, then what are we victims of? For every executive who chases a secretary around the desk, there is a secretary who dreams of marrying an executive and not having to be a secretary anymore.[27]

Romantic entanglements do occur at work, and women are just as baffled by this situation as men are. What, for instance, does a woman do if she is attracted to her boss? She worries about what her coworkers will think if she enters into a romance with him. She may wonder if it is worth it for her to date her boss if others will assume that her success came about not because of talent but because of romance, or even worse, because of sexual favors she offered in order to get a promotion.

A Look Ahead

Some experts say that the problem of sexual harassment in the workplace is not likely to be solved in courtrooms and with the exchange of money and reprimands. A simpler solution lies in changing the workforce so that women are no longer such a small minority. Sexual harassment consultant Frieda Klein claims that the problem diminishes as women become less of a minority in the workforce—once 30 percent of the workers in a department, an assembly line, or a company are women.[28] Assuming the present trend continues, and more and more women work at a full range of jobs, sexual harassment may well become less of a problem in the years ahead than it is today.

4

Sexual Harassment
in the Schools

I t begins in tension in the nape of her neck. The hallway seems longer as she walks past the row of guys. She walks a little faster and holds her books closer. The guys aren't touching her, but with that all-too-familiar smirk, they are degrading her. It's impossible to prove the guys have been harassing her. They leave no marks or trace, except the flushed cheeks of the girl and the belittled rounding of her shoulders as she pretends to ignore them.   —Aki Morizono, 12th grader[1]

School is supposed to be a safe place. When parents send their children off to school, they may worry about them getting good grades, making friends, and having enough fun to learn to love learning. Only recently, it seems, are parents beginning to wonder if they should worry about their children experiencing molestation, humiliation, and defeat in their classrooms.

According to a 1993 nationwide survey commissioned by the American Association of University Women Educational Foundation, four in five American teenagers have experienced some form of sexual harassment at school. The majority reported suffering harassment from schoolmates, but one-fourth of the girls and one-tenth of the boys said they had been harassed by teachers and other school employees. One in ten said they have been forced to commit a sexual act beyond kissing during school hours.[2]

Sexual harassment in schools takes several forms, but for the purpose of this discussion, we will divide it into two broad categories: harassment by teachers toward their students, and harassment by students toward their peers. In both scenarios, the risk is high for misunderstanding and false accusation. If harassment has occurred, however, the results can be devastating because the victim is probably too young to just shake it off or to understand that it is the other person's fault.

Sexual harassment from high school peers is humiliating and can have a lasting effect on a student's grades and self-image.

Teacher's Pet

Imagine that you are an eighth-grade student with a young teacher who is the most popular and exciting teacher in the school. This teacher—Mr. X—seems to genuinely care about each of his students, but he also seems to particularly care about you. He is the type of person who does a lot of touching. When you do something that pleases him, you are rewarded with a hug. Sometimes he comments about what you're wearing, your hair, the way you walk, and your smile. He seems to watch you and seems determined to help you become the best, brightest, most attractive person you can be.

And, of course, you're thrilled about the special attention—until one day after school, when his good-bye hug suddenly seems too long, too intense. His hands feel strange and frightening—they are lingering too low on your back. You've recently been reading about sexual abuse, and your parents have talked to you about it. When you push Mr. X away that day, he looks hurt and confused. And you begin to wonder if you were overreacting, imagining things. What a horrible thing to accuse someone of, especially someone you like as much as Mr. X. You try to apologize, but he doesn't touch you again—ever.

In the next few weeks, it seems as if you can't do anything right, at least not in Mr. X's class. He seldom calls on you in class discussion, and when he does, he is critical of your comments. Your grades begin to slip. But nobody seems to notice anything wrong. Mr. X seems to be paying a lot of attention to another student now. Maybe, you figure, your work just isn't as good as it used to be. You vow to work harder. You finish that semester insecure and worried about your ability. You also wonder if you're just a prude and feel grateful that you never said anything to your parents or to another teacher or a counselor about Mr. X. You'd feel awful if you'd ruined his reputation.

Is it possible that such an experience could affect you for a long time? What is different about this situation if you are a boy rather than a girl? If Mr. X were Ms. X? In the situation described, the teacher doesn't actually molest the student, but does he harass her?

In 1992, the head coach of a girls' basketball team in Minnesota was fired after being accused of sexual harassment by eight of his players. The girls accused the coach of behavior—including hugs and kisses on the forehead—that offended them and made them feel uncomfortable. Physical touching is not unusual from coaches or among teammates, whether they're boys' or girls' teams. In this case, what the girls found most offensive was not the physical contact, but rather the coach's sense of humor, which contained sexual innuendo.

The ex-coach claimed that his jokes were no more offensive than those commonly told by most people. "I'm not going to walk through life on pins and needles because I'm afraid to say anything," he said. "I like to have fun, but I don't mean to insult anyone. There's a lot of basketball terms that could be taken two ways."[3]

Many people worry that we have gone from not taking accusations of sexual harassment seriously enough to the opposite extreme of taking them too seriously, thus putting all teachers at risk and making them afraid to express any warmth toward their students. In addition, such accusations give a powerful weapon to students who

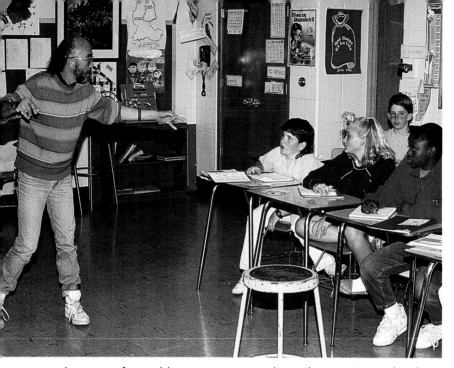

In terms of sexual harassment, a popular and energetic teacher has a great deal of power over his students, but he is also vulnerable to false accusations from disgruntled students.

are out for revenge against a teacher (for bad grades, for ignoring them in class, or whatever). A teacher's career and life can be destroyed by false accusations. Even when she or he is proved innocent, that person's reputation remains tarnished.

Totally false accusations, however, will probably continue to be rare. And many cases of sexual harassment in schools are extremely blatant. A teacher has power simply by being an adult working with young people. Add to that the fact that teachers are in the unique position of evaluating student performance and giving grades that become part of a student's permanent record. Some students will do almost anything to get good grades, or to get praise and attention. They are more vulnerable to suggestions by the teacher that kissing, petting, or even sexual intercourse, are acceptable behavior between teachers and students. To resist might mean failure in school.

Despite numerous studies, no one knows exactly how many teachers harass or molest students, because these incidents so often go unreported. But sexual misconduct is the primary recorded reason for taking away a teacher's certification.[4]

Teachers who abuse students often start out as the most outstanding in their field. They often give their students extra help and attention and only later reveal their dark intentions. As Utah attorney Doug Bates puts it, "If you are going to prey on children successfully, you've got to be someone kids like to be around, parents trust, and the community respects."[5]

Of course, it is not impossible for a teacher to genuinely care about—or even fall in love with—a student, especially at the college level. But more often it is the student who falls in love, and for teachers to take sexual advantage of students is an abuse of power. Adolescent students are particularly vulnerable because, although they are still kids, their bodies and their feelings are becoming adult. The students may be convinced that what is happening at school is a "love affair" when it is actually sexual harassment.

Clear Cases of Abuse

Women's rights groups have claimed at least a few major victories in the more blatant cases of sexual harassment in schools. For example, in February 1992, a former Georgia high school student, Christine Franklin, changed the law of the land when her case came before the U.S. Supreme Court. Lower courts had thrown out her lawsuit because they said she was not entitled to win money damages. The U.S. Supreme Court unanimously disagreed. They ruled that students who suffer sexual harassment and other forms of sex discrimination can seek money damages from schools and school officials for violating civil rights.

The Court's decision surprised and delighted women's rights groups, who had not expected the justices to disagree with the stance of the Bush administration. President Bush had warned that providing for money damages could expose schools to "potentially massive financial liability" without directly affecting how well they comply with civil rights laws.[6]

Christine Franklin had claimed that Andrew Hill, a sports coach and teacher, started harassing her in 1986, when she was a 10th grader. His alleged offenses included asking her about her sex life and whether she would have sex with an older man, forcibly kissing her on the mouth, and calling her at home to ask her out on dates. The situation seriously worsened during her junior year. Franklin says that Hill interrupted classes on three different occasions to ask her teacher to excuse her. He then took her to a private office, where he had sex with her.

The road to the Supreme Court and eventual vindication was not a smooth one. Franklin claims that other teachers and school administrators were aware of Hill's harassment of her and other female students but did nothing about it. In fact, she was discouraged from pressing charges against Hill. Before she brought the lawsuit, Franklin filed a complaint with the U.S. Department of Education, which found that she had been subject to harassment. But the department dropped the case because Hill had resigned by that time, and Franklin's former school had finally established a grievance procedure.[7]

Franklin's case against her teacher is fairly clearcut, and Hill's behavior was grossly inappropriate and damaging. How much less damaging is it when the sexual harassment is more subtle?

Consider the following story. Although it recounts harassment from long ago, many college students tell of similar experiences today.

> It happened almost the first day of college. The campus smelled of autumn leaves and I was excited as I walked to my first literature class. I was only eighteen . . . .

> The instructor seemed like a nice, middle-aged man. Going over the course contents with us, he said we'd be discussing novels, short stories, and various magazines, especially *Fortune* magazine [which, he said] "has articles about money, business, etc. It's the kind of magazine a woman would never read." My head jerked up, I stared at the professor. I read that magazine. I looked around and realized I was the only woman in the class.

> Lit 101 met three times a week and we had to read out loud from various books. The men read from Steinbeck, Hemingway, Melville, but the professor always assigned me Mickey Spillane. These were trashy, sexy, detective stories. So once a week I had to stand and read things like "They shot her through the navel so it wouldn't mess up her body," followed by a description of her bust line. Some of the men would snicker, some would leer, but the smirks were the worst. Stony-faced, choking back rage, I stood there reading, determined not to let my humiliation show.

All I wanted was to get a decent grade and get out of that class. The course was required or I might have given up. On the days I had literature I wore a green, full-length coat and if we were going to read I left my coat on. I felt humiliated and put upon, but in those days we were not allowed to feel put upon. That was forty years ago, but I still remember the positions and faces of the men who were sitting around me and I still feel my rage . . . .[8]

In this example, the student's peers played a major role in harassing her. Led by their professor, they created a hostile environment in that classroom. In many other cases, sexual harassment takes place among peers, without any adults involved.

Peer Pressure with a Twist

Jill Olson was an eighth grader when she first became aware of sexual harassment at school. Sometimes boys would "spike" girls (pull down their pants) or make crude sexual comments. When she got to high school, Olson found that the harassment was just as bad.

Among other things, some male students created a list of the most sexually desirable female students, complete with detailed descriptions of the girls' bodies and sexually explicit remarks about them. Olson was on that list and complained to school authorities, but nothing was done about it until she filed a complaint with her state's Department of Human Rights.[9]

One of the problems in fighting sexual harassment is that people often don't recognize it. They see it as an inevitable part of being a student, and they don't realize that there are legal remedies. Even high school girls who are targeted by harassment can get caught up in the atmosphere at school and make the mistake of accepting sexual harassment as normal behavior. Later, when they've become more mature and aware, they are likely to feel differently and wish they had fought back.[10]

Students often shrug off sexually degrading comments and unwanted touching in school halls and classrooms as teasing. And such behavior is not one way. Girls harass boys as well, although boys may be less likely to find it offensive and degrading. And boys are certainly less likely to feel physically threatened.

Most girls feel they have to put up with a certain amount of harassment, either by laughing it off or ignoring it. Teachers and administrators often don't seem to care about such behavior. School authorities are far more likely to intervene when they hear racist comments or sense tension between racial groups than when they observe evidence of sexual conflict. And some students report that a few teachers and administrators even participate in the harassment by laughing or making their own comments.[11]

What is the ultimate result of sexual harassment for young women? Their self-esteem is lowered when they are constantly bombarded with messages that they are sex objects, second-class, weaker, and less effective than their male counterparts. Eventually these women may begin to accept such sexist labels for themselves. Harassment can affect women academically too. Their goals become diminished, and they tend to choose more traditional routes for themselves. In other words, young women who experience sexual harassment are less likely to achieve their full capabilities.

"I was upset every day," Jill Olson says. "I got to the

point where I didn't want to go to school." Most of her friends told her she was "overreacting," so she felt isolated and alone. "It was terrible, because I felt I was going against that whole entire school.[12]

Are We Going Too Far?

The recent spotlight on sexual harassment has led some parents and students to complain that schools are going too far in cracking down on alleged offenders. Furthermore, not everyone agrees that it is possible or even desirable to try to control relations between male and female teenagers with laws and lawsuits. Teasing, taunting, and pursuing might appear offensive and damaging as seen through adult eyes. For most teenagers, however, exploring and testing the boundaries between genders is harmless.

By the time students get to college, dating and sexuality become more serious matters, and gender conflicts can intensify. College campuses create an atmosphere of independence and change. Students get caught up in an earnest effort to see how they will fit into the world as adults. The transition from adolescence to adulthood is rarely smooth, and puzzling over sexual relationships consumes a large amount of time and energy during this period.

Incidents of sexual harassment and assault are a major concern on college campuses all over the country. No school, however, has addressed the issue more strongly —and more controversially—than Antioch College in central Ohio. The goal of its Sexual Offense Policy is to empower female students to become equal sexual partners with males. In order to ensure "100 percent consensual sex," incoming freshmen are instructed that it isn't enough to ask someone if she'd like to have sex. Male students must get permission every step of the way: "Can I kiss you?" "Can I unbutton your blouse?" "Can I take your blouse off?" "Can I touch a breast?" And so on.

Critics say these guidelines diminish sexual experience, especially the surprising and spontaneous aspects of it. Even more unsettling, the policy reinforces the outdated notion that it is the man's role to initiate sex and the woman's role to apply the brakes. One female Antioch student says, "I think it encourages wimpy behavior by women and [the idea] that women need to be handled with kid gloves."[13]

The issue of female victimization is important to young women. Rape frequently occurs on college campuses. But many young feminists argue that "rape crisis feminists" have exaggerated the problem of date rape and stirred up a kind of hysteria on college campuses. Katie Roiphe, who at age 25 published a landmark book called *The Morning After: Sex, Fear, and Feminism on Campus,* is often called a traitor to women for suggesting that rape has become too loosely defined. Should the definition of rape include any sexual experience a woman perceives as negative?

> The image that emerges from feminist preoccupation with rape and sexual harassment is that of women as victims, offended by a professor's dirty joke, verbally pressured into sex by peers. This image of a delicate woman bears a striking resemblance to that '50s ideal my mother and the other women of her generation fought so hard to get away from . . . But here she is again, with her pure intentions and her wide eyes. Only this time it is the feminists themselves who are breathing new life into her.[14]

Many teenage boys are confused about what is and is not permissible in their relationships with girls and often discuss it with each other.

Many boys and young men are more confused than enlightened by sexual harassment policies. Is it okay, they wonder, to approach a girl in the hall and comment on how beautiful she looks that day, to touch her shoulder, to pursue her for a date?

One high school junior put it this way:

> What is sexual harassment? You can't define it, let alone prove it. Many of the women at our school flirt a lot, and I haven't seen any of them charged yet. Also, you cannot consider foul language or remarks to be sexual harassment, because a lot of the time it's coming from both sides. Our school recently adopted a sexual-harassment policy, and consequently several innocent guys have got-

ten into trouble for casual remarks. This policy only causes more stress in the relationship between men and women by stereotyping men as overly aggressive pigs and women as whiny, helpless victims. A better solution than a sexual-harassment policy would be to encourage women to be more assertive. Most of the girls who keep getting harassed are the ones who refuse to stick up for themselves. Also many of the ones who retaliate just put down all men in general, without regard for the nice ones. If women made an effort to act like men's equals instead of like victims, many harassers wouldn't be able to get away with it. —Philip Ziermann[15]

Although sexual harassment cannot be tolerated in schools, examples of overreaction in this area exist as well. How far can we go to ensure one person's right to a harassment-free environment without taking away another person's right to freedom of speech?

Graydon Snyder, a religion professor for more than 30 years, saw his reputation permanently tarnished due to harassment charges. "It's humiliating," he says. "People hear about sexual harassment, and they suppose I went around pinching students." What was Snyder's offence? He recited a story from the Talmud, the writings that make up Jewish civil and religious law, involving a rape that was described as "unintentional." The story offended a woman in his class because she said it justified brutality toward women.[16]

Without question, sexual harassment does occur on college campuses, but in the attempt to prosecute all cases of serious abuse, a few legitimate academic discussions may end up silenced.

5

SEXUAL HARASSMENT IN EVERYDAY LIFE

"Hostile environments" don't exist only in the workplace and schools, of course. The streets and even our homes can be hostile as well. Many women feel unsafe walking, jogging, or biking alone—especially if they live in a city. Women bear the brunt of a full range of behavior in the streets, from leering and whistling to obscene and threatening remarks to actual physical contact. Of course, men occasionally report similar forms of harassment, but unless the harasser is also male, men are less likely to feel threatened. After all, men don't fear being raped by women.

When harassment creeps into one's own home, however, no one is immune to fear. Intrusive phone calls are probably the most common form of harassment in the home. In many cases, the person calling remains silent and then hangs up, or perhaps tries to intimidate the victim with heavy breathing or sexual remarks. Even a question as seemingly harmless as "What are you wearing right now?" can be not only invasive but terrifying if the victim is at home alone, if the caller has used the person's correct name, and if the calls have been repeated. Some callers find the anonymity of the phone irresistible and will say things they would never say in person.

Explicit threats, especially of a sexual nature, are not un-common on the phone. And the victim never knows how serious the caller is.

Sexual harassment by strangers in everyday life makes people feel vulnerable to the unknown attacker, never sure when, where, or how he or she might strike. Women frequently feel threatened by violence, real or imagined. Their fear is heightened by news reports and other media attention to violence against women. In addition to living with fear, many women have become extremely sensitive to being treated by strangers as sex objects rather than as human beings—and they are angry.

Everyday Abuses of Power

Thirteen female tenants won an $800,000 settlement against their San Francisco landlord in 1991. He had ig-nored their complaints of sexual harassment by the apartment manager he employed. According to court records, the manager grabbed one woman between her legs and on her breast and threatened another woman with eviction if she invited men to stay overnight. He told women who had trouble paying their rent on time that he would wait for it more patiently if they would model lingerie for him. The women were all single moth-ers and very vulnerable—financially and emotionally—to his threats.[1]

Landlords hold a position of power over people, espe-cially in this age of homelessness. Many people feel pow-erless against someone who can evict them from their homes. Of course, eviction on the grounds of sexual re-jection is illegal, but fighting legal battles takes time and money. Where does a victim of landlord harassment live

"Helping" professionals who abuse their power can be particularly damaging to those seeking their help.

in the meantime? What if she or he has children? Many people are only one month's rent away from homeless-ness. In this situation, a person will do almost anything to avoid eviction, and an unscrupulous landlord knows that.

Another common form of harassment that involves an abuse of power occurs in the offices of doctors, psychia-trists, social workers, clergy, and other "helping" profes-sionals. Patients or clients enter into such a relationship because they need help, but if exploited, they can end up more damaged than when they initially sought help. This kind of harassment ranges from demeaning comments all the way to sexual assault and rape.

Why don't such victims of this kind of exploitation speak up immediately and avoid further problems? Because they are in a uniquely vulnerable position, many people feel extreme pressure not to offend a medical professional or others in positions of power. How difficult is it to file an official report against a physician for what a woman thinks was sexual innuendo or inappropriate touching? How can she prove such an offense when there were no witnesses? Can she even be sure enough of what happened to face skeptical questioning and probing into her own character?

Furthermore, patients sometimes become emotionally attached to, or even infatuated with, their doctor or therapist. The majority of people in helping professions are ethical, and, finding themselves in this situation, would end the relationship and refer the patient to someone else. An unethical person, however, may exploit the patient's feelings.

Why does this happen? Many experts blame attitudes in this society that confuse sex with power. Some professionals and their victims are culturally programmed to become involved when sexual feelings arise, to fall into the roles of powerful, attentive professional vs. helpless, sometimes love-struck patient. In her book *Talking Back to Sexual Pressure,* Elizabeth Powell explains:

> The whole culture encourages men to challenge women's intimate boundaries. Our society discourages men from learning to empathize with women [and] also programs women to respond positively to men in power, to feel . . . flattered by the advances of a male professional.

Police officers are also in a position of power and some officers have been known to sexually exploit suspects, male and female. Men standing together on a street can be stopped and questioned with offensive implications about their sexual orientation. Women have reported being arrested for minor offenses, such as a series of unpaid traffic tickets, brought into the police station, taunted, and even strip-searched (the process of searching all openings in the body for evidence or weapons). Of course, most police officers are ethical professionals, but it takes only a few frightening examples to make everyone fearful of the very people who are hired to protect and defend us.

Stalkers

"Stalking" (pursuing someone secretly and deliberately) not only invades a person's privacy, but also presents a continuing threat of physical violence, even murder. We frequently read about celebrities being stalked. For example, a female fan of TV talk show host David Letterman wrote him intimidating letters, claimed to be his wife, repeatedly broke into his house, and could only be stopped by arrest and imprisonment. Television actress Rebecca Schaeffer was not only stalked but ultimately murdered by her "admirer," John Bardo.

Men as well as women have found their lives disrupted by the unwelcome attention of either a stranger or someone they know. The movie *Fatal Attraction* was one of the most talked-about films of 1987. The victim in this case was a strong, seemingly competent man, but his life was nonetheless slowly and mercilessly shattered by a disturbed woman who claimed to love him.

Nineteen-year-old John Bardo, an obsessed fan of actress Rebecca Schaeffer, was charged with killing her in 1989. He was found guilty of first degree murder and received a life sentence without parole in December 1991.

Sometimes love is not even involved. Stalkers, who are often mentally ill, may only have a strange desire to invade someone else's life, perhaps out of envy, vengeance, or misplaced concern. For victims, such harassment can include receiving letters and phone calls, being followed or watched, and having personal belongings taken, destroyed, or tampered with. Often there is very little the police or anyone else can do about stalking because it is so subtle and difficult to prove.

If violence is not explicitly threatened, can't this kind of harassment simply be ignored? No, because it is still an invasion of privacy. The cumulative effect of uncertainty and the violation of privacy can take its toll even if the victim is in no apparent physical danger. As "Carol"—the

Hostile environments exist in the home, the street, the park, as well as in schools and workplaces.

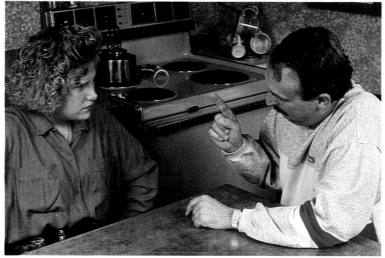

victim of a stalker in Minnesota—can attest, it's the little things that drive you crazy.

The ordeal for 55-year-old Carol began in December 1991. She could tell that someone was coming into her office when she wasn't around. Small objects in her office were moved around; heads were broken off a bouquet of flowers; her office nameplate disappeared. In one photo of her, the smile was scratched off her face, while in another, her eyes were scratched away. Her home and office phones rang frequently with anonymous calls.

Although nothing of major importance happened, she definitely felt threatened. Carol said that she worried about being considered crazy if she reported what was going on. After several months, she finally discovered the culprit, one of her coworkers. When she reported him to her employer, Carol became the subject of investigation and her job was put in jeopardy.

Many of her male superiors and coworkers sided with the accused harasser. Carol became the butt of office jokes about sexual harassment. Coworkers who tried to defend her were similarly ridiculed and felt their jobs threatened. Even after obtaining evidence, such as the man's incriminating phone records and videotapes of him in her office, Carol was told to dismiss what was happening as harmless and to get treatment for her stress-related health problems.[3]

She ended up resigning from the job she had held successfully for 18 years, while her harasser continued in his position with only a two-week suspension. Finally she filed a double lawsuit against the individual for stalking her and against her employer for sexual harassment. At this writing, the results are still pending. "It has to do with power," Carol says. "Some men can't handle a professional woman becoming too powerful. The kind of harassment I endured is the crazy part of a backlash against women in the workplace."

During the first few months of 1992, in response to several high-profile cases, lawmakers nationwide began to focus on stalking as a unique and insidious form of psychological harassment, usually of a sexual nature. As a result, more than 20 state legislatures—including Carol's home state of Minnesota—passed antistalking laws. These laws defined a repeat offense of this kind as a felony instead of the less serious misdemeanor it had been. Typically, these laws define stalking as the willful, malicious, and repeated harassment of another person. Some laws require a direct threat of violence; others require only that a victim *senses* that a threat has been made.[4]

Dr. Rick Schuman, a psychologist and founder of the Center for Victims of Crime and Trauma in Encino, California, says the stalking victim's suffering has been minimized long enough. "You don't know what the other person is capable of and how far they may go," says Schuman. "It is one of the most terrifying experiences you can go through. It is an ongoing crisis. Psychological rape."[5]

Home
Not all sexual harassment is perpetrated by strangers. Many women consider the kind of treatment they have received at the hands of friends or family members as damaging as anything a stranger might do. For instance, adolescent girls can be deeply embarrassed by a relative's teasing comments about their developing bodies or sex appeal. Such behavior can, if severe enough, consti-

tute sexual harassment. Some women are given continuous, relentless messages by their fathers and later by their husbands that they are inferior and have few rights because of their gender. This, too, can be sexual harassment. A woman's self-confidence can be undermined, for instance, when her ideas and opinions are automatically dismissed as dumb, childish, or typically feminine. Is this an overreaction? Many people say no, that battering and child abuse often occur, day by day, in subtle ways and that abusive power is still the issue.

But it is important to question if and when we are going too far, labeling as sexual harassment just about anything unpleasant or annoying related to sex and gender. Some people accuse feminists of overreacting, especially radical feminists like Andrea Dworkin, who has written extensively about male domination. She has written, for example, that:

> Until about 20 years ago, men did what they wanted and called it what they liked. They decided all meaning and value. They could describe sex as conquest, violence, violation, and themselves as rapists (without using the word) because they were never accountable to us for what they said or did. Men were the law; men were morality; men decided; men judged. Now we have pushed our way out from under them, at least a little. In the last two decades, feminists have built a real political resistance to male sexual dominance, i.e. to male ownership of the whole wide world; and it is clear that we are not saying no because we mean yes. We mean no and we prosecute the pigs to prove it.[6]

6

DEALING WITH
SEXUAL HARASSMENT

I've never experienced a hint of harassment. And I don't know anyone who has. I always wondered [why]. I'm not a cold person; I'm a flirt. I never wore a man's suit, never tried to hide my femininity. I've probably never been harassed because people see my strength of character. I've always been self-confident because I knew I could get another job. If you do a good job, nobody will question your sexuality. I'm a freight train; I don't deviate. I'm going too fast to look at the landscape. If you put it in first gear and keep going, you will be recognized. You don't have to be masculine, just indispensable.   — Liliana Nealon, vice-president, New York
branch, Union Bank of Switzerland[1]

If you're insecure, it comes out. Like an animal, you can see vulnerability. Some people are good at finding weakness. But nobody has power over you unless you allow them to have it. Me, I plow on through. If you're in my way, that's your problem. If I can't achieve my goal one way, I'll find another way. Important thing to remember:

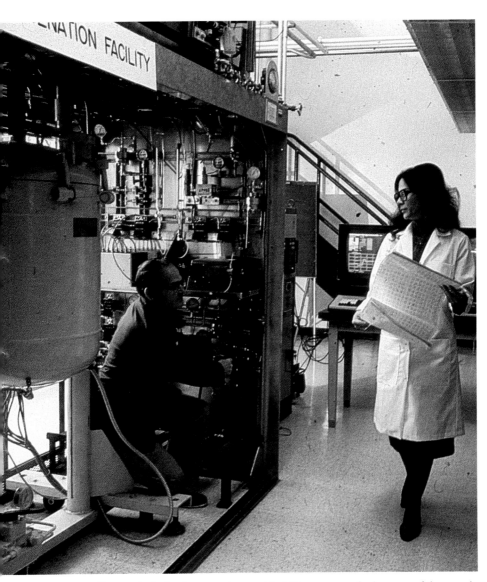

Some victimization can be avoided if a woman feels powerful enough to say, "Back off, bub."

You create your limitations. It doesn't have anything to do with biology.   — Valerie McDowell, co–owner/president, William Allen Co., New Jersey[2]

The above businesswomen express a point of view that we hear more and more as the dust settles from the Thomas-Hill controversy. If women expect to compete with men in school and at work, should they expect a perfect environment? Should they expect to be protected, or should they be expected to take care of themselves?

Clearly, some victimization can be avoided. Again, sexual harassment is not about sex, it is about power. If women act powerless at work, they're more likely to be taken advantage of. As Gretchen Morgenson wrote for *Forbes* magazine, "Women are more powerful than the sex harassment peddlers will have you believe. A woman's power is not in her ability to bring a harassment claim, it's in her ability to succeed on her merits. And to be able to say, 'Back off, bub.'"[3]

There is considerable evidence that your own assertiveness can improve your environment. People with high self-esteem tend to recognize disrespectful treatment and are more likely to assert themselves against harassment.[4] But it's more than a matter of self-esteem and assertiveness. Why do so many people become victims? One reason is that the rewards held out to victims of sexual harassment—including job security, promotion, acceptance, and status—are hard to resist.

Of course, it's possible to strive for these rewards without risking harassment. What, then, differentiates one group from another? Those who are most vulnerable to sexual harassment seem to share certain characteristics, including a lack of confidence, fear of failure, poor self-image, inexperience, and gullibility (not knowing whom to trust).[5]

Vulnerability, however, does not justify exploitation. Furthermore, in most cases women are not playing victim but truly are victimized, no matter how self-confident or competent they may be. Although considerable progress has been made, there is little doubt that situations of unequal and abusive power do still exist.

If you think you are a victim of sexual harassment, recognize what is happening and try to determine why. Ask yourself the following questions:

Are you experiencing behavior that is sexual in nature and unwelcome?

Is it directed at you because of your gender?

Your own confidence and assertiveness can improve your environment.

Make it clear to the offender that his (or her) behavior is unwelcome.

Is it happening deliberately or is it accidental?

Is it repeated over and over?

Have you said or indicated that you don't like it?

Do you participate in any way or initiate the behavior?

If all your answers to all these questions point to a clear case of sexual harassment, tell the harasser to stop. Although federal law defines sexual harassment as "unwelcome" behavior, the offender must know that his or her behavior is, in fact, unwelcome. Otherwise, the behavior will not be considered sexual harassment by any school, government agency, or court.

As important as it is, however, speaking up can be difficult. A nationwide survey conducted in 1991 by two professors at the University of St. Thomas in Minnesota revealed that, among women who said they had been victims of sexual harassment, only 34 percent told the harasser to stop. Only 2 percent filed a formal complaint.[6]

When confronting the offender, be specific about what behavior you want stopped—the way he or she talks to you, the physical contact, the looks or gestures, or whatever it may be. If you write a letter to the offender, describe the offensive behavior and the dates it occurred. Don't be combative or threaten legal action, but say that you know your options. Offensive behavior often stops once the harrasser knows how you feel.

If this doesn't end the offensive behavior, then what? For too many people, the next step is silence—often fueled by denial of the problem. Unfortunately, ignoring the problem rarely results in its disappearance. All studies show that victims are very reluctant to say or do anything about the situation. Unless they do, however, the harassment will probably continue. Many employers and school officials think they have no harassment problems because no one has made a complaint.[7]

Keep a written record of all harassing incidents and of any complaints you make against the harasser, school, or company. Include in this record: where the incident occurred, the date and time, what happened, what you said, how you felt, and the names of any witnesses or others who have been harassed by this person.

Do you have to file a lawsuit right away? Not at all. Because of the emotional and financial cost, going to court is a last resort. You will probably want to make an informal complaint first. This means seeking out someone who is trusted and knowledgeable—a teacher, a supervisor, a manager, or a mentor. You could also go to an affirmative action director, a women's center, or a human resources officer. Seek support and get the best advice available to you. Sexual harassment is not something to deal with all alone.[8]

If the harassment occurred at school and school officials have not tried to stop it, you can file a complaint with the Department of Education's Office of Civil Rights. The department will ask you to fill out a complaint form or write a letter within 180 days of the most recent incident. Usually within three months, the department will decide if harassment has occurred. If, after an affirmative decision, the harassment is allowed to continue, the school district can lose its federal funding.[9]

If the problem persists in spite of unofficial complaints, you may want to file an official charge against an individual, school, or company. Sexual harassment *is* illegal. Title VII of the Civil Rights Act of 1964 prohibits discrimination on the basis of race, color, religion, national origin, and sex. Harassment is a form of sex discrimination. If you decide to take legal action, try to find a lawyer who will take your case on a contingency basis. In other words, the lawyer will not demand payment right away but he or she would get a percentage of any money you are awarded as a result of your case.

To take legal action, you must file a complaint with the United States EEOC within 300 days of the harassment. The EEOC will review your claims. If the commission finds them to be valid, you can sue the school or offender in federal court. You may be offered a settlement, such as money or other compensation, and assurances that the harassment will stop. Or you may have to go to court. If so, be prepared for a long battle. As with rape cases, victims of sexual harassment may be questioned about their conduct, manner of dressing, sexual history, and other personal matters.[10]

To file a charge, the two major agencies to notify are:

Equal Employment Opportunity Commission (EEOC)—check the U.S. government section of your telephone directory

Human Rights Commission—check the state government section of your telephone directory

7

THE ROAD AHEAD

A re we making progress in combating sexual harassment? If you were to ask Teresa Harris that question, her answer would be a jubilant "yes." Six
years ago, this Nashville, Tennessee, woman quit her job
in despair. Her boss had made lewd suggestions to her,
teased and threatened her, and made remarks like, "What
do you know? You're just a dumb-ass woman." Harris
spent six long years sitting in courtrooms, trying to con-
vince judges that she had been sexually harassed. Lower
courts ruled that her boss's behavior was not "severe"
enough to be in violation of federal law. Harris never expected what happened next.

In October 1993, her case prompted the U.S. Supreme
Court to take a fresh look at sexual harassment. In a sur-
prisingly quick and unanimous decision, the highest
court in the land told lower courts, employers, and the
American public how seriously to take women's claims
of sexual harassment. In *Harris v. Forklift Systems* the
Court decided that the behavior of Harris's boss was in
violation of the law, and, as Justice Sandra Day O'Connor
wrote in the decision, "Federal law comes into play before the harassing conduct leads to a nervous breakdown."[1]

Addressing the issue of sexual harassment can create an atmosphere of equality and hope.

Helen Neuborne of the National Organization of Women (NOW) Legal Defense Fund said, "We are thrilled with the court's strong message that when women suffer sexual harassment, they will be treated exactly the same as any other group discriminated against based on race, religion, or national origin."[2]

Harris's case represents the trend—since the Hill-Thomas confrontation—toward more women stepping forward and more American citizens taking their complaints of sexual harassment seriously. And nobody is immune to accusations, including a United States president.

In the spring of 1994, President Bill Clinton suddenly found himself embroiled in a sexual harassment lawsuit. Paula Jones, a woman who had worked as an administrative assistant in Arkansas's industrial development commission when he was governor of the state, accused Clinton of sexual harassment. At this writing, the investigation of her case against Clinton is underway. He denies all charges and says that the lawsuit is part of the effort by his conservative opponents to prevent his reelection. But regardless of his prominent position, and in spite of his impressive record in support of women and their rights, it is still a matter of his word against hers.

During the early 1990s, many people—men and women alike—gained a keener understanding of the issue of sexual harassment. American citizens have struggled with their own definitions and examples, compared them with others, and engaged in debates. They have become increasingly aware of the dangers involved in trivial, exaggerated, or downright false accusations, but they are also convinced that the problem is real and that constructive change will benefit everyone.

Forcing this complex issue into everyone's home, school, and workplace may well have created more tension and confusion about male/female interaction, but addressing the issue openly has also created an atmosphere of hope that we will work things out and become a more humane country as a result.

As summed up by Jonathan Alter in a *Newsweek* commentary:

> Men are on notice that true sexual harassment has a price . . . Women know that if they try to destroy a man's career for some flimsy reason . . . they can expect withering cross-examination. Major social change is inevitably awkward, even excruciating . . . But there has always been something messy about democracy. And it's always better to face the truth and feel the pain than never to have bothered at all.[3]

Endnotes

Chapter 1. A "New" Social Issue

[1] Rebecca Sisco, "Sexual Harassment—Girls Fight Back," Minnesota Women's Press, October 9-22, 1991, 1.

[2] Susan Brownmiller and Delores Alexander, "From Carmita Wood to Anita Hill," *MS,* January/February 1992, 70.

[3] Ibid., 71.

[4] Jill Smolowe, "She Said, He Said," *Time,* October 21, 1991, 38.

[5] Andrea Sachs, "9-Zip! I love it!" *Time,* November 22, 1993, 45.

[6] Barbara Kantrowitz, "Striking a Nerve," *Newsweek,* October 21, 1991, 34.

[7] Jeanne Cummings, "Women Nearly Triple Seats in U.S. Senate," *St. Paul Pioneer Press,* November 4, 1992, 11A.

[8] Nancy Gibbs, "Office Crimes," *Time,* December 9, 1991, 116.

[9] Sarah J. McCarthy, "Cultural Fascism," *Forbes,* December 9, 1991, 116.

Chapter 2. Male/Female Roles

[1] Jon Tevlin, "Why Women Are Mad As Hell," *Glamour,* March 1991, 206.

[2] Laura Shapiro, "Why Women Are Angry," *Newsweek,* Oct. 21, 1991, 41.

[3] Ibid., 43.

[4] Tevlin, 209.

[5] Susan Faludi, *Backlash,* (New York: Crown Publishers, 1991), 393.

[6] Shapiro, 41.

[7] Ibid., 43.

[8] Ibid., 41.

[9] Karen Pennar, "Women Are Still Paid the Wages of Discrimination," *Business Week,* October 28, 1991, 35.

[10] Mary Ann Roser, "Girls Hurt by Gender Bias in Classroom," *St. Paul Pioneer Press,* February 12, 1992, 1A.

[11] James C. Dobson, "Biology Determines Gender Roles," in *Male/Female Roles: Opposing Viewpoints,* Neal Bernards & Terry O'Neill, Eds., (San Diego: Greenhaven Press, 1989), 20.

[12] Francine D. Blau and Marianne Ferber, "Economics Determine Gender Roles," in *Male/Female Roles: Opposing Viewpoints,* 47.

[13] Kantrowitz, 34.

Chapter 3. Sexual Harassment in the Workplace

[1] *Gibbs,* Nancy "Office Crimes," *Time,* October 21, 1991, 53.

[2] Ibid.

[3] Mary Corey, "Men Say Sexual Harassment Tables Are Turning," *Star Tribune,* August 30, 1993, 1E.

[4] Ibid., 9E.

[5] Ted Gest and Amy Saltzman, "Harassment: Men on Trial," *U.S. News and World Report,* October 21, 1991, 40.

[6] Gibbs, 53.

[7] Susan L. Webb, *Step Forward: Sexual Harassment in the Workplace* (New York: MasterMedia Limited, 1991), 19.

[8] Leigh Montville, "Season of Torment," *Sports Illustrated,* May 13, 1991, 60.

[9] Gibbs, 63.

[10] Jill Smolowe, "An Officer, Not a Gentleman," *Time,* July 13, 1992, 36.

[11] Eloise Salholz, "Deepening Shame," *Newsweek,* August 10, 1992, 30.

[12] Ellen Goodman, "Tailhook Story Moral: Getting Away with It," *St. Paul Pioneer Press,* February 12, 1992, 12A.

[13] Gilbert Lewthwaite, "Top Officer's Fall Closes the Book on Tailhook Debacle," *St. Paul Pioneer Press,* February 20, 1994, 2A.

[14] Gest & Saltzman, 38.

[15] Gibbs, 54.

[16] Sara Hammes, "Dealing with Sexual Harassment," *Fortune,* November 4, 1991, 148.

[17] Gibbs, 63.

[18] Naomi Munson, "Harassment Blues," *Commentary,* February 1992, 50.

[19] Gest & Saltzman, 40.

[20] Gibbs, 64.

[21] Gest & Saltzman, 40.

[22] Ibid.

[23] Gibbs, 64.

[24] Gretchen Morgenson, "May I Have the Pleasure . . . .," *National Review,* November 18, 1991, 37.

[25] Ibid.

[26] Jane Gross, "Suffering in Silence No More," *New York Times,* June 13, 1992, A16.

[27] Gibbs, 63.

[28] Morgenson, 41.

Chapter 4. Sexual Harassment in the Schools

[1] "Insights in Ink," *Star Tribune,* Education Publications, March 1992, 1.

[2] Theresa Monsour, "Survey Finds Sex Harassment Rife in Schools," *St. Paul Pioneer Press,* June 2, 1993, 1A.

[3] "Nicollet Coach Fired," *Star Tribune,* February 13, 1992, 5B.

[4] Elaine Whiteley, "Nightmare in Our Classrooms," *Ladies Home Journal,* October 1992, 76.

[5] Ibid., 80.

[6] "Schools Can Be Sued for Sex Bias," *Star Tribune,* February 27, 1992, 1A.

[7] Ibid., 5A.

[8] Jeannine Crane, *Sexual Harassment, Women Speak Out,* Amber Coverdale Sumrall & Dena Taylor, Eds. (California: The Crossing Press, 1992) 61.

[9] Rebecca Sisco, "Sexual Harassment—Girls Fight Back," *Minnesota Women's Press,* October 9-22, 1991, 1.

[10] Ibid.

[11] Ibid.

[12] Ibid., 10.

[13] Sarah Crighton, "Sexual Correctness," *Newsweek,* October 25, 1993, 54.

[14] Ibid., 55.

[15] "Insights in Ink," 2.

[16] Dirk Johnson, "'Word Cops' Monitor a Classroom," *Star Tribune,* May 13, 1994, 4A.

Chapter 5. In Everyday Life

[1] Barbara Kantrowitz, "Striking a Nerve," *Newsweek,* October 21, 1991, 40.

[2] Elizabeth Powell, *Talking Back to Sexual Pressure,* (Minneapolis: CompCare Publishers, 1991), 129.

[3] Ellen Tomson, "Bit by Bit, Terror Becomes Overwhelming, *St. Paul Pioneer Press,* June 26, 1992, 1A.

[4] Ibid.

[5] Ibid., 8A.

[6] Andrea Dworkin, Introduction to *Sexual Harassment: Women Speak Out,* Amber Sumrall & Dena Taylor, Eds. (California: The Crossing Press, 1992), 7.

Chapter 6. Dealing with Sexual Harassment

[1] Gretchen Morgenson, "Watch That Leer, Stifle That Joke," *Forbes,* May 15, 1989, 72.

[2] Ibid.

[3] Ibid.

[4] Powell, 115.

[5] Beryl Black, *Coping with Sexual Harassment* (New York: The Rosen Publishing Group, 1987), 65.

[6] Anne B. Fisher, "Sexual Harassment, What to Do," *Fortune,* August 23, 1993, 86.

[7] Powell, 114.

[8] Ibid.

[9] Amy Saltzman, "It's Not Just Teasing," *U.S. News & World Report,* December 6, 1993, 74.

[10] Ibid., 127.

Chapter 7. The Road Ahead

[1] Andrea Sachs, "9-Zip! I love it!" *Time,* November 22, 1993, 44.

[2] Ibid.

[3] Jonathan Alter, "Why There Isn't a Better Way," *Newsweek,* October 21, 1991, 45.

Resources

Equal Employment Advisory Council
1015 - 15th Street NW
Suite 1220
Washington, DC 20005
202-789-8650

Equal Employment Opportunity Commission (EEOC)
1801 L Street NW
Washington, DC 20507
202-663-4264 or
1-800-669-EEOC

Equal Rights Advocates
1663 Mission Street
Suite 550
San Francisco, CA 94103
415-621-0672

Men's Rights Inc.
P.O. Box 163180
Sacramento, CA 95816
916-484-7333

National Association for Female Executives
30 Irving Place
5th Floor
New York, NY 10003
212-477-2200

9to5
National Association of Working Women
614 Superior Avenue NW
Room 852
Cleveland, OH 44113
216-566-9308 or
1-800-522-0925

Nation Organization for Men (NOM)
11 Park Place
New York, NY 10007
212-686-MALE

National Organization for Women (NOW)
1000 - 16th Street NW
Suite 700
Washington, DC 20036
202-331-0066

NOW Legal Defense and Education Fund
99 Hudson Street
12th Floor
New York, NY 10013
212-925-6635

Bibliography

Alter, Jonathan. "Why There Isn't a Better Way." *Newsweek,* October 21, 1991, 45.

Amiel, Barbara. "Feminist Harassment." *National Review,* November 4, 1991, 14-15.

Bernards, Neal & Terry O'Neill, Eds. *Male/Female Roles: Opposing Viewpoints.* California: Greenhaven Press, 1989.

Black, Beryl. *Coping With Sexual Harassment.* New York: The Rosen Publishing Group, Inc., 1987.

Brownmiller, Susan and Dolores Alexander. "From Carmita Wood to Anita Hill." *MS,* January/February 1992, 70-71.

Crighton, Sarah. "Sexual Correctness." *Newsweek,* October 25, 1993, 52-56.

Faludi, Susan. Backlash. New York: Crown Publishers, 1991.

Fisher, Anne B. "Sexual Harassment, What to Do." *Fortune,* August 23, 1993, 86.

Galen, Michele, "Out of the Shadows," *Business Week,* October 28, 1991, 30-31.

Gest, Ted & Amy Saltzman. "Harassment: Men on Trial." *U.S. News and World Report,* October 21, 1991, 38-40.

Gibbs, Nancy. "Office Crimes." *Time,* December 9, 1991, 52-64.

Gibbs, Nancy. "An Ugly Circus." *Time,* October 21, 1991, 35-47.

Hammes, Sara. "Dealing with Sexual Harassment." *Fortune,* November 4, 1991, 145-148.

Kantrowitz, Barbara. "Striking a Nerve." *Newsweek,* October 21, 1991, 34-40.

McCarthy, Sarah J. "Cultural Fascism." *Forbes,* December 9, 1991, 116.

Montville, Leigh. "Season of Torment." *Sports Illustrated,* May 13, 1991, 60-65.

Morgenson, Gretchen. "Watch That Leer, Stifle That Joke." *Forbes,* May 15, 1989, 69-72.

Morgenson, Gretchen. "May I Have the Pleasure . . . " *National Review,* November 18, 1991, 36-41.

Munson, Naomi. "Harassment Blues." *Commentary,* February 1992, 49-51.

Pennar, Karen. "Women Are Still Paid the Wages of Discrimination." *Business Week,* October 28, 1991, 35.

Powell, Elizabeth. *Talking Back to Sexual Pressure.* Minneapolis: CompCare Publishers, 1991.

Sachs, Andrea. "9-Zip! I love it!" *Time,* November 22, 1993, 44-45.

Salholz, Eloise. "Deepening Shame." *Newsweek,* August 10, 1992, 30-36.

Saltzman, Amy. "It's Not Just Teasing." *U.S. News & World Report,* December 6, 1993, 74.

Shapiro, Laura. "Why Women Are Angry." *Newsweek,* October 21, 1991, 41-44.

Sisco, Rebecca. "Sexual Harassment—Girls Fight Back." *The Minnesota Women's Press,* Vol. 7, No. 14, October 9-22, 1991, 1.

Smolowe, Jill. "An Officer, Not a Gentleman." *Time,* July 13, 1992, 36.

Smolowe, Jill. "She Said, He Said." *Time,* October 21, 1991, 38.

Sumrall, Amber Coverdale & Dena Taylor, Eds. *Sexual Harassment: Women Speak Out.* California: The Crossing Press, 1992.

"Talking Dirty." *The New Republic,* November 4, 1991, 7-8.

Tevlin, Jon. "Why Women Are Mad as Hell." *Glamour,* March 1992, 206-209.

Webb, Susan L. *Step Forward: Sexual Harassment in the Workplace.* New York: MasterMedia Limited, 1991.

Whiteley, Elaine. "Nightmare in Our Classrooms." *Ladies Home Journal,* Oct. 1992, 74-81.

Index

Acknowledgments

American Media Incorporated, Video Training Products, cover, 30, 39, 78; DoD Still Media Records Center, 7; Du Pont Company 75; Geraldine Ferraro, 20; © Richard B. Levine, 23, 77; Minneapolis Police Department, 33 (bottom); © National Geographic Society, courtesy, The Supreme Court Historical Society, 12; National Aeronautics and Space Administration (NASA), 19; Reuters / Bettmann, 10, 11, 34, 35, 38; Skjold Photographs, 2, 26 (bottom), 54, 62, 66, 70 (bottom), 83; Nancy Smedstad / IPS, 15, 26 (top), 43, 46, 51, 70 (top); UPI / Bettmann, 33 (top), 69.